3-16-79

Beside the Sea of Glass

Beside the Sea of Glass

The Song of the Lamb

DANIEL BERRIGAN

Photographs by Frank Kostyu

1978
The Seabury Press
815 Second Avenue
New York, N.Y. 10017

Copyright © 1978 by The Seabury Press, Inc.

Photos on pages 37 and 47 by Tom Lewis; on page 65 by Robert Hollister
Davis; on page 70 courtesy Lookout Mountain Air Force Station.

Printed in the United States of America

Library of Congres Catalog Card Number: 77-93989
ISBN: 0-8164-2174-9

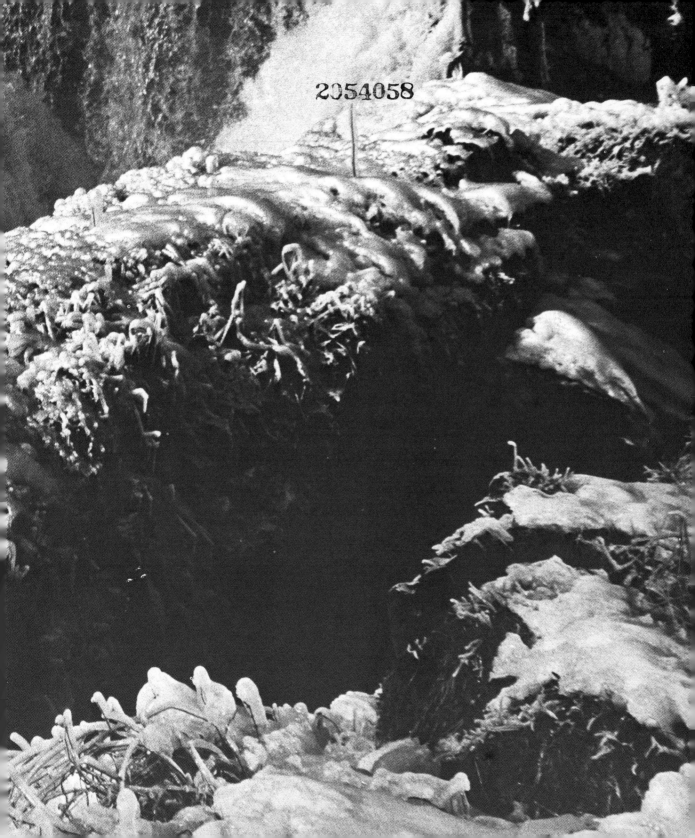

Then I saw what looked like a sea of glass, mixed with fire. I also saw those who had won the victory over the beast and its image, and over the one whose name is given by a number. They were standing by the sea of glass, holding harps that God had given them. They were singing the song of Moses, the servant of God, and the song of the Lamb:

> *"Lord, God Almighty,*
> *how great and wonderful are your deeds!*
> *King of all nations,*
> *how right and true are your ways!*
> *Who will not fear you, Lord?*
> *Who will refuse to declare your greatness?*
> *You alone are holy.*
> *All the nations will come*
> *and worship before you,*
> *because your righteous deeds are seen by all."*

Revelation 15:2–4

INTRODUCTION

In February of 1977 a group of us were in the Alexandria (Va.) city jail, meditating and discussing the book of Revelation. It dawned on me that ours was a perfect setting for such an enterprise. After all, hadn't many early Christians ended up in just such places, for just such offenses against law and order? Hadn't they been forbidden to preach in the name of the Risen One—forbidden, that is, by the civil authorities, to whom that name and that event were understood as a mortal danger?

We had undertaken something not very different from that offense, saying nothing more momentous than this: the State has no right to build and maintain an arsenal of nuclear weapons that threaten the life of the planet. To underscore our resistance to this grotesque program, we had poured our own blood on the pillars of the building and chained ourselves to its doors. For this, we were of course jailed. We had expected nothing else. It was not the first time; nor would it be the last.

So, Alexandria, here we were.

I thought it might be a good thing, especially for myself and those who were in jail with me and possibly our friends "outside," if I were to set down these reflections concerning a prayer that

unexpectedly moved us all, a prayer virtually unknown to us up to that time. (One, indeed, that I think will be equally unfamiliar to others.) It is a prayer that one passes by easily, its language at once unfamiliar and overfamiliar, phrases that trip easily off the tongue, having to do with things beyond our ken or indeed our interest. Nevertheless, the prayer stopped us short. It seemed, perhaps due to our circumstance, charged with a terrible energy and beauty; a prayer almost like an instrument of torture, stretching us, adding inches to our moral understanding—if only given the chance, given some reflection.

I wanted to begin these reflections with a story that, to my mind, helps the prayer come alive.

The Prayer of the Lamb, we are told in Revelation, is recited (shouted would be a better term) "by the sea of glass." The phrase intrigued, teased, puzzled me. Since boyhood, I have loved the sea, gotten lost (and found) by the sea, recouped my spirit there, listened and learned there, at times even been reborn there. In prison it seemed as though my poor pate had become a conch, resonant with the sound of the surf—that sound whose deprivation was a punishment indeed. I have always marveled at that terrifying body and soul of ceaseless motion, of secrets, solitudes, furies. I have known all its moods and changes: a sea of storms, sea of savageries, the comparative calm of a living and reflecting being, a sea of enticements, of great command and surpassing dignity, a king of nature on a high throne.

But one thing I have never known, and I doubt indeed whether such a thing exists at all, this side of the veil. Namely, the marvel described by Revelation as the setting for the Prayer of the Lamb: a "sea of glass." That, I said to myself, will bear some thought.

Or maybe not thought; maybe less thought and more imagining. For it must have been imagined in order to exist at all.

Imagine! A sea of glass! And they say this is an inspired word, an inspired image. Truly?

Truly, in the Bible; but not so commonly understood in religion. I remember reading that an eminent Jesuit was forbidden to pursue a certain line of speculation, as being "too hot for the present." The authority so instructing him then added, either in sardonic spirit or consoling humor: "Why don't you take to writing something like poetry for now?" The advice, however aimed, is revealing. Imagining, writing poetry, telling stories, is commonly thought of as an inferior occupation, recommended because it is, after all, quite harmless.

A sea of glass? We are discomfited; the image cannot be verified. Neither can it be quite dismissed.

I wanted to tell a story about that story (thereby undoubtedly compounding the offense of a God who, at times, dares not to be serious). A story that might tell how this wonder came to pass. How the sea, that mighty creature of myriad faces, of a thousand days and nights, of sunrisings and settings, of what we have come to name, conceding the issue of change to the sea alone, "sea changes"; this sea that never once in the memory of humans has repeated its vesture, mood, voice, coloration—how it became, finally and forever, a "sea of glass."

That would be the first part of my effort: setting the stage, so to speak, for a study of this wondrous and powerful prayer. After that, I would take the words of the prayer in hand, telling lovingly and in detail what it came to mean to my friends and myself. (For I wish to speak for them too, and thereby to thank them for those

days together and for the conscience and friendship that led us, together and so often, to jail.)

No one of us, of course, has ever in our lives stood by such a sea as the prayer describes, indeed, takes for granted. And, quite probably, we never will, on mortal feet. We have, on the contrary, walked another sort of sea: the tricky storm-dark waves of this century, this world, where the strongest resolve often turns to water and the calmest waters rise like a phalanx of furies at our approach.

And that, as they say with a sigh, is life.

Might I also add this? I am of no mood to offer an apology for opening these notes with the story of the sea that turned to glass. Indeed, it seems to me that we have stepped upon shaky ground; the connection between imagination and faith quite eludes us. Stories may be all right for children (or for reproved but reformable Jesuits). We say it with a sniff. But give us adults who are serious and straight from the shoulder and with no nonsense, the meat and potatoes of the Ten Commandments of Almighty God or the Six Commandments of Holy Mother Church!

This we say, with a straight face.

Then we open (rather rarely, it must be admitted) the New Testament and are immediately shaken. What is this? Jesus tells so many stories! Indeed, if he is to be taken seriously, it is clear that he was not always and everywhere serious, but sometimes playful and humorous and ironic and not above a dig at this or that overweening religious stiff upper lip! Have we missed something here?

Indeed, he loved a story as much as the Russians or Irish (those masters of the trade) do. Was it because he had first imagined the world itself, that wildly improbable mad place where even we, the maddest hatters of all the living fraternity of unlikelies, might exist?

[14]

And in that world, was he not also bound on that imaginative ragged journey of the heart, which is as much his trip as ours? Neither more, I think, nor less.

He tells so many stories. Indeed, if the love of God and of one another is at the heart of things, then he told his parables, his tales, in season and out, to bring that love home to us in ways that mere commands never could—its warmth, horizons, discipline, its many faces. He seemed to know, far beyond our twilit capacity, that when the mind is won or the will engaged, we (all that is in us, all that we might be) are by no means won. ''What indeed of the heart?'' He never ceases asking.

What indeed? I begin with a story.

HOW THE SEA GREW CALM AS GLASS, AND WHEN AND WHY

The waters seemed always to be asleep, inward turned, from top to bottom, transparent, colorless, just next to nothing.

More, content to be that way, uncomplaining as spilt milk, soft-footed as air, yielding as the will of a lover.

But the waters, if the truth were known, were none of these things—spilt milk, lover, air. Especially, the waters were not asleep. They could more accurately be compared, if one were willing to look and look, to the watchful look back of an open eye.

And they had a voice: I am able to show the fact, since what follows actually occurred. And when one has spoken and been heard, it cannot but be inferred that the speaker speaks.

The waters said to the Creator: "You have made us a creature lower than the air, the most mollified, malleable, manageable of all creatures. Do you know what you have done? You have made us the shame of all creation, a do-nothing, a go-nowhere, a pure and metaphysical passivity. Sometimes we are not sure we even exist at all; we must gather our wits and furrow our brows and think, who are we anyway?"

It was a gentle, scarcely audible complaint and even God must stretch low and close his eyes in concentration to hear, pledged as he is to attend to the voice and needs of all his creatures.

Pooooorraaahh poooooorraaahhh was the nearest one could get to it, as though the waters were drinking of themselves or weeping of themselves or merely thinking of themselves.

But he heard. And all he said was: "Just wait." Bending low over the waters and speaking, so to say, into their very ear. "Wait," was all he said.

And the waters waited. They were used to waiting, under duress as they were. They veiled their many eyes and sealed their many lips, where he had placed his finger for a moment when he whispered, "Just wait." In spite of this, we are not to think that patience came naturally to the waters, any more than it comes so to tigers or great eagles; or for that matter to redwoods or bogs or chance rocks on the roadside. I know there are sayings to that effect, "Patience comes naturally." But like most popular assumptions, this one rests, I think, on the excusing of one's own impatience, or a sense of superiority, of one's being neither tigerish nor doltish in one's mind. Or perhaps on congratulation for being patient by virtue, where other creatures lie there or stand there or wander there, patient by heaven's decree.

In any case, it should be explained that the waters were a still pool and went nowhere. This was their makeup, temperament: calm. Whether they encompassed a vast sea in extent or trembled in a single drop—a jewel at the throat of creation—or are best described by something in between, this I cannot say. For the reason that the waters themselves did not know. Nor did they care, for that matter.

They were purely self-conscious. Whether of a drop or an ocean, whether sweet or salt, warm or cold of pulse, they were—water.

Conscious, too, that the God who whispered to them was a God of water.

Conscious that the land surrounding them was a land of water.

Conscious that the sky above was a sky of water.

All things sweetly, endlessly referred to themselves, reflected in themselves, coming from themselves, returning to themselves.

And in this they may have been right. Who is to say?

But, right or wrong, this was how it was: watery heart, limbs of water.

Indeed, as we say commonly to this day, of pool or ocean or river or great lake indifferently—a body of water.

The waters waited, as instructed.

It could even be said they endured.

For they were, after all, more or less willingly in service to all other beings.

The tiger came down to their margin like a blazing sunrise and drank its full.

The sun leapt on them from overhead, roaring with thirst. Then he sank into the waters like a burning brand, exultant, savage, wounding. The roots of great trees crept eagerly across the earth

and put their lips to the waters like a moving ground of serpents and eels, drinking, drinking, very misers above a pot of gold.

Humans came too, adults and children. They bathed and laughed and drank and washed their clothing, all in exercise of a claim whose gesture was the beat of their limbs and the sound of their voices, a heartfelt denial of death uttered in the very element of death. They came to the waters dry as stones and departed wet as fishes, and all indifferent as stones or fishes. As though the waters were, not mother and father of all beings, but senseless, valueless, without limit or exhaustion, divisible as worms, dumb as the scattered rocks.

And the storms came. They tortured the waters hours upon end, twisted their gentle limbs upon a rack, struck them with nine tails of lightning, flailed, fragmented them, until like a distrait mind, spread-eagled in agony, the waters found voice to cry out once more to the Creator: "Do you know what you have made of us? Do you know what they are doing to us?" The voice was fainter now, hardly to be heard, the faint cry of the drowning.

And the Creator bent low over the dying waters and spoke into their ear. He said only: "Wait." Only that. Then, a little longer, "Wait."

And the waters waited, obedient even unto death. . . .

And one day, the waiting was over.

The creator cried out like a clap of thunder, like the voice that, before anything was, firmament or stars or sun or moon or beasts or flying creatures or humans, made all things to be. He cupped his hands and put them to his lips, and from that tremendous trumpet cried out three times: "NOW. NOW. NOW." The last great "NOW" fell like a bolt of lightning.

Then the rains began. They fell and fell. And the world, like a great barren earthen bowl, began to fill. First imperceptibly, gratefully, harmlessly. Then more and more, up and up and up.

No longer were the lips and tongues and mouths of creation tipping the waters, an always available cup, to their own direction and heedless comfort; the lips of tigers, the tongues of trees, the mouths of children.

Now the waters were claiming the earth.

All creatures had held the waters prisoner to their whims, their appetites.

Now the waters, like a legion of barefoot warriors, fanned out in all directions, scouting, ravening.

The tender flowers of the field went under; rose, cowslip, aster, hydrangea, herbs, spices, omnivorous weeds, together with the small animals that fed off them and made their homes at their roots—moles, mice, bugs, together with the flying creatures one seldom sees in daytime. They went, sleeping, into watery night.

The appetite of the waters grew. The long wait of God was over. Water was king. The waters said in exultant pride of heart: The earth is no more, or soon will be no more. When I have swallowed the world, I will reach up and seize the sun and cast him forever into my lowest dungeon—that one who in the day of my humiliation drank me at a draught.

. . . and lambs of the field, calves, foals, the water plucked them from their mothers' side. A last pitiful baaaah, bleat, blattt, whinney, they were no more.

And their dams, ewes, mares likewise, and great stallions and of course, prior to these, in order of lesser excellence, mules, cows, bullocks, zebras too, goats and lesser sheepish creatures, not knowing a flood from a fetlock, they went under. Wondering, maybe, wooly and ruminant, what all this watery rough and tumble might mean, passing as they did from green fields to green waters, seeing no great difference worth remarking. The following too were drowned:

giraffes

baboons

zebras, already mentioned,

lions and

cheetahs, the exotic beasts seen only by most of us in national zoos, visitors whom we visit, so to speak, now they were set free, like those who captured them, into a larger, indeed, a final freedom.

Then, drowned in a transport of terror, men and women were no more.

Masterful they had been, keepers of creation, tillers of fields, weavers, cunning workers in metals and fabrics, quick in all kinds of invention and improvisation, builders of barns and towers, cathedrals and temples. Boastful, too, beyond measure: "Who is like us in all the world," they would cry, "our towns, our megalopolises, our armies, our derring do, our treasures and museums, our GNP, our space programs. . ."

Whole families took to the roads, aimless, beleaguered, wandering this way and that as the land receded and hope grew dim. Some of them even clambered aboard the vast rumps of the elephants who stood trembling like half-uprooted oaks in the rising waters. Those immense spaces seemed to the hopeless people like the top of a sugar loaf mountain or a breathing continent. For a time, at least, space without limit!

[24]

Only for a time.

It was wonderful and terrible to see how that vast area of cloudy ash grey, at first empty as Labrador, slowly grew into a suburb, then became a heaving, teeming city slum.

And then, the last day of Pompeii; the poor land whales trumpeted and trampled about in a frenzy. They went under together, animals and people, a loud, trailing, stentorian hardly human ALASSSS, a barnacle infested rock in a raging tide.

Steely, single-minded, straight as a file of braves, the waters marched on, Galway Athlone Clara Tullamore Portarling and Dublin Kildare Tullamore Portarling. That was the way they marched if you happened to be Irish. Or, if you were in America for some reason, it was New York to San Francisco, like a finger's snap or a war whoop. Or in three short, mad minutes, Dar es Salaam to Lagos; the waters met in the great African plains, standing eye to eye, fifty feet tall, a crazy wild embrace, the kiss of sharks. Everywhere, everywhere, first a broiling foam-capped spine, then the spine broken; a snorting rip tide, a flattening out. All, all gone, the world gone under.

The Creator's great thunder clap NOW resounded throughout the planet forty days and forty nights. NOWNOWNOWNOW-NOW it went on and on like a Comanche battle cry, the waters parting the land, scalping their verdure, drowning them whole, swallowing, swallowing with a cat's silken cruelty, a cat's smile. Carving their way, a knife of waters, a hatchet blade raised and lowered, lowered and raised.

Thirty-nine and three-quarters days it went on, that blind, furious mist and fog and spray.

Not a human left, not a speck of land to comfort the eye, if there had been an eye. Nothing left north, east, south, west, but that limitless, raging jungle and tangle of waters. What a world it was! The most patient doddering whale in creation would surely have turned its belly up and breathed its last in sheer watery boredom.

Look though. It was now thirty-nine and seven-eighths days, toward dusk of the longest, weariest, wettest devastation of all.

Look sharply. Something—a mote in the eye? A mirage compounded of tears, a hopeless hope, a waterlogged brain?

The sight of anything at all would have been strange, a relief, a monstrous shock to the brain.

And here, in that dense and blundering and sodden world, the strangest sight of all.

A boat.

But a boat, you would have said, only in the widest and most generous of terms.

A chip on a flood, to speak more accurately.

The waters stood there and blinked and scratched their wild and wooly locks. They were sure of themselves beyond telling, reaching mightily from end to end of creation. They almost reached out to this, so to speak, S. S. Impertinence and pulled it down like a cockleshell.

Except for one thing.

For the Creator had been sitting quietly until that moment on Mt. Olympus, hunched up in the door of his cave, his arms resting on his knees, his beard dripping and waving like a tangle of seaweed. Thirty-nine and seven-eighths days. Oh he never lost count at all! You could tell it by the unwavering look of those blue eyes, that had never closed for all those days and nights, bluster or fog, wind or tide. Had you been as vigilant as he, you would have known that something was up now. Rain wasn't going to fall forever. Something else was to come.

The little ship hove in sight. God's head went up with a jerk. You would have thought he'd heard something, a creak of the tiny planks, a sigh in the halyards. His eyes narrowed. He stood up now, tremendous! He waved his trident once and shouted, WAIT!

Then the waters, somewhat set back, saw something staggering to the mind.

With his other hand the Creator was upholding the little boat. Like a child's hand, his hand. At arms's length, he held it tight and trim, a smidgeon of water, and the perky little ship, like a homemade walnut shell sailboat a child makes and launches, slightly tipsy and off course in a pail of water.

It could now be seen, moreover, that the little boat had a name painted on its stern in large careful Gothic: S. S. Salvation. Its port of call was Mt. Olympus; its builder, owner, navigator and captain, a former landsman rather suddenly turned seaman—Noe.

Now he could be seen too, his long beard waving over the rail in the spanking breeze, a blue cap on his bald head broidered in large careful Gothic—CAPTAIN: S. S. SALVATION.

And around him, close as peas in a pea pod, were his wife and fourteen or fifteen sons and daughters, their husbands and wives and sons and daughters and their spouses and children to the ninth and maybe even the tenth generation.

And then, in pairs all peering over the boat's railing (for on Mt. Olympus they had come up the gangplank two by two): giraffes and elephants and zebras and gazelles and mountain goats and lowly donkeys and great tossing stallions, with butterflies balancing on their ears.

And creatures also of the lower kingdoms:
grey, pensive mice and moles, earthworms; also
birds of paradise and peacocks pulsing like rainbows and,
if your eyes were sharp, even moths and insects and blank-faced
owls, blinking and crying in the sudden clearing light,
"Who's there? Who's there?"
Also, I almost forgot,
monkeys and chimpanzees, a little apart and, as usual, making fools
of themselves.

All these and more (you could name them better than I) stood, sat, swayed, fluttered, tomfooled, perched, lounged, cawed, mewed, bellowed, sang, hehawed, cockadoodledoed, neighed, roared, there at the railing of the little boat.

The hand of the Creator was under them all, between them and the waters of oblivion. His breath was gently in the sails, so that the S. S. Salvation never sailed far from its port of call, Mt. Olympus.

Only think of it; all those weary days at sea were no more than the circle of a walnut shell around the edge of a pail of water, a child's breath blowing against its toothpick mast and sail.

That was when the Creator said with a wave of his trident, "Wait." It was the fortieth day since he had said, "Now." And he said, "Wait." And the waters which had advanced fierce, warlike and stealthy, turned about and crept back on all sides from the mountain. They were like warriors whose mission is over.

Thus, a widening circle of land appeared. And God took hold of the hawser attached to the prow of the S. S. Salvation and fastened the end with a sailor's knot to the peak of Mt. Olympus. And the little boat beached gently in the receding tide.

Then the Creator sat down, his knees drawn up, and watched,

a smile on his lips, as Captain Noe lowered the gangplank.

Two by two they came, down to earth again, wife and sons and daughters and their children to the ninth or the tenth generation, followed, in the order they had taken going up, by all the animals and birds and crawling creatures and insects.

The children, moreover, were carrying in their hands all kinds and manners of fauna and flora, down to the least meager invisible points of life, lowlier even than the ticks and lice, the single curled cells that lay hidden in the dirt that nourished the plants. These all came down to earth in the hands of children, all safe and sound.

Then the Creator called the peacocks and birds of paradise to one side, and instructed them as follows: "Take wing immediately across the rejoicing sky and trace there, with your brilliant wings and shimmering tails, a Rainbow, a kind of love knot, joining into one element, earth and sea and all that dwelt between."

Then to the waters, kneeling chastened and silent at his feet, he said: "You have tasted your great power. You have been the lowliest, then mightiest of all. You must now dwell in the middle ground. I promise you, never again will you be humiliated among creatures. Dwell now at peace in the world. Love the earth that supports and contains you, the rocks that give you voice, the children that (as I have instructed them) from henceforth will give thanks as they drink from you." Then he turned to the vast assembly of creatures, from the least to the greatest, waiting expectantly in concentric circles, scarcely moving, scarcely breathing.

"Be at peace among yourselves," he commanded. His voice was like the sound a great horn makes at dawn, summoning, summoning. "I give you this charge," he thundered, "be at peace. The waters have receded, the earth is renewed; all, all is in your hands."

Turning to the children he said, "Be also at peace; more, be signs of peace one to another and to all beings."

He turned to the adults, men and women, who stood in the outermost circle, like the upturned tips of the petals of the flower of creation. "I have snatched you from the waters," he said, "against all expectation, I have set your feet on dry land once more. Now I give into your hands the governance of the world. Look how my promise is arched above you in the heavens." (And indeed it was, it was a celestial circle above their earthly ones; it was the ribbon of the basket, woven all of light, containing the flower that was themselves.) "No more death by water," he thundered.

"But you must know, there are other deaths; death by fire, death by sword, death by malice, the twist of the tongue, the twist of the blade; wars, race set against race, hatred of brother for brother. May you taste none of these. May you never desire to taste them, the ingredients of the stew of hell."

Oh he was somber in that brilliant setting; he looked through and beyond them, and grew silent. The men and women, too, stood silent; the children looked about them in bewilderment; the circles of creation grew still, all things were like the inward heart of a flower, when the skies cloud over.

Then the Creator shook his mighty shoulders, as though ridding himself of the burden of memory or the burden of the future (bleak indeed, the times bloody, men furious and deranged, the world sodden, this time with human blood.)

Or perhaps he was merely shivering in his damp clothing.

In any case, his countenance brightened again, his eyes rested like a benediction on his people, he stretched out his arms to them. "A new command I give you," he cried, "that you love one another as I have loved you."

His arms lowered slowly, he took up his trident where it lay on the earth. And he passed among them like a father, with a word here and a silence there. But mostly in silence.

So out of travail and death, goodness came to all things, for the sake of all.

And the charge of the Creator, and the knot of light he tied in the heavens, they hover there in the sky, dwell here on earth, under which, in which, all things dwell. If we grow blind to them, if we go deaf, it is to our utmost peril.

And the Creator went off to his cave high on Mt. Olympus where, deep in meditation, it is said he dwells to this day.

BY THE SEA OF GLASS: THE PRAYER OF THE LAMB

On the face of it, a more unlikely prayer to fit our present situation could hardly be imagined. We are not at the "end of things" (not even at the end of our rope). We're by no means a great multitude of every nation and tribe; only a few firebrands, momentarily snuffed by the huge paw of the State. Nor have we undergone martyrdom, or many of its analogies or stages. Not for us that wolfish litany of contempt and torture, vile putdown, which Paul tells us was his lot in preaching the Gospel. No, we live in a kind of obscene twilight, a holding tank of various wounded and sick piscine specimens, floating or kicking feebly for a while here, between the hook and the skillet—victims of the elemental pollution we all breathe.

We are Christians. We are Americans, after the fact, some

being pleased to put the strange prefix *post-* before each of these. We are also humans, and the *post-* prefix edges toward that word with a horrid lurch, every time a rivet is added to the ominous hull of a nuclear submarine, or a nuclear bomb goes off in atmosphere or depths.

We are really trying to prevent the death of all peoples. That threat is by no means an idle one. Our political leaders have repeated the threat, and have pointed a monitory finger time and again at the nuclear arsenal that gives it substance. So are they all, all honorable men. Their honor, which they claim is derived from the electorate and from us (the Christian community), consists in this audacious, beefed-up threat: to dispose of the world in a manner which God has literally never imagined or threatened.

Hence, our trouble, a lifelong matter, literally a matter of life and death. Hence, also, the pressing urgency of this prayer.

The claim to be Christians, as we understand it, demands that we confront the claim of the State (a claim which ultimately lays hands on us)—to be silent, to walk in lockstep, to hand over our scripture, our sacrament, to the vile uses of military czars. To bless them—by doing precisely nothing. To stifle the voice of Christ in the world. To collaborate in normalizing the abnormal. To conspire behind closed doors and drawn shades, with the odious militarization of conscience. To help "absorb" the mystery of the Lordship of Christ into the bowels and brain of Caesar.

Hence, it seems to me, the point of this prayer which, strangely enough, speaks of none of these things; neither of Christian conduct and will in face of the State, nor of the call to resistance, nor of the price to be paid, nor least of all of a blueprint of ethics. Nothing. Yet, in the circumstance of its utterance, certainly all these matters enter closely.

[36]

Resistance, courage, patience, above all the love that animates and warms the will. They are all there, in those who shout the prayer, who have walked through this world's hellish gauntlet, and prevailed.

A prayer that could only be spoken by those who stood together in the struggle, worshipped together, raised families, lived in poverty, endured mistreatment and fury and, finally, to crown it all, death. Many voices, which are finally a single voice. The single voice is also that of Paul:

> For it seems to me that God has given us the very last place, like those condemned to die in public, as a spectacle for the whole world of angels and of humans. . . . For Christ's sake we are fools . . . we are weak . . . we are depised. . . . To this very hour we go hungry and thirsty; we are clothed in rags, we are beaten; we wander from place to place; we work hard to support ourselves. When we are cursed, we bless; when we are persecuted, we endure; when we are insulted, we answer back with kind words. We are no more than this world's offscourings; we are outcasts in the world, to this hour.

The voices, the prayer, come to us from the "other side" of death. Hence its strangeness. Hence also its point. Spoken on the other side, it is meant to be prayed by us, who are cursed or blessed by dwelling on this side. Are we not then the other side of that other side? Is not their prayer, the prayer of the Church triumphant, our prayer as well?

It must be. Hope cannot live on in a vacuum, unless we are to plant our hope like a dead stick stolidly in "things which are seen," which is to say, unless we are to put Christian hope to an untimely death.

[38]

It must be our prayer. In spite of the fact that the prayer is denied, reviled, contradicted, made sport of, mistranslated every hour of every day—by the powers and dominations, by Church and State, by law courts and schools and think tanks. Yet, the prayer needs to be verified, insisted on, repeated, persisted in, learned by heart, shouted in unison, enacted, pondered. It exists indeed only to the degree that it makes sense to Christians, that they stretch their wills and voices to its understanding. To make of it their credo; to make of eternity their native ground (as of this world their proving ground). In the manner also of those who first uttered the prayer: our friends, our brothers and sisters in the spirit and in the flesh. Those whom death cannot bury out of mind, nor the imperial State seduce or betray.

As they pray they stand by a "lake of glass."

At every hour his angel of deliverance comes to us. In noise and stench and foolish anger, and the ever-flowing spate of damaged lives. In the evidence of breakup all around—broken bones, broken hopes, splayed carcasses of sound beginnings. In this jail. Where we must dwell. Not a lake of glass, you understand. But in a desert of fire. The ever present demons within. Enticements. Despair. Depression of spirit. Disabused hopes. And even with one another; a certain paralysis, outreach cut short.

Is the *via negativa* the way, a dead end? Is it the only street still passable in the modern world? A one-way street leading straight to chaos?

The prayer would deny it. "All manner of things shall be well." We must, by sheer grit of faith, live in that future, live it until it is as vividly present as any beloved possession, any loved one, could well be. We join those for whom all manner of things *is* well; they join with us, for whom all manner of things is intolerably unwell.

The future and the present join hands—barely, but truly. The meeting is incandescent, an ecstasy in the midst of torment.

You can understand the prayer, its audacious character, only if you understand this: the prayer is everywhere and at all times denied. It has little place in this world. The powerful may mouth it, but their acts give the lie to their words. The violent may try it for size, but deception lies heavy on the air. The immaculately tailored diplomats may stand at attention while it is intoned, but their respect is charged with servility, spurious mourning. Very few can say such a prayer—and mean what they say.

It is the possession of those who have come through "the great travail," have refused "the mark of the beast," have, like John, been exiled for "witnessing to that word." Indeed those who first chanted the prayer, by "the lake of glass," were precisely the ones who, in another scene, "cry out for justice from beneath the altar" (Rev.6:9).

If we understand the world with that bitter and exalted wisdom which faith entails, we may become worthy of the prayer—to say it, to mean it. . . .

Are those who pray it with exaltation, in the vision of God, also those who carry into eternity the stigmata of Jesus? And at the same time, the wound of injustice—unhealed, unrepaired? They are.

The conclusion is clear—eternity demands justice, a righting of wrongs. The martyrs are not palliated by their victory. They retain, like a cicatrice on glorified flesh, the memory of their trials, torture, the malevolence of judges, the bloodthirst of mockers, the absurd charade of justice that condemned them. How long, O Lord, will you delay?

[41]

Until the end. Everything that goes around, comes around; until then, God answers. But his answer is silence. There is no accounting for him, literally. He defies all the faking fakirs, the hucksters of his word, the kingmakers who would make him, in their own debased image, a magical healer, a murderous surgeon. He is silent. He is silent in courtrooms; he stands at the bar of every grand inquisitor, presumed guilty, accused, without recourse, the poor man or woman, lost in the labyrinth, a Kafkaesque nightmare of injustice.

How long, O Lord, will You delay?

In this cell block a drugged zombie sleeps the days and nights away, a breathing vegetable. His eyes show a flicker of light only momentarily. He walks the length of concrete and back again. Wall to wall—a figure of his life. His accusers have won; their net has fallen on him. He will walk the length of life granted him, ghetto wall to wall, until he simply falls over. For him we can do very little. Neither our scripture, our cigarettes, our well-meant words, our attempts to draw him into converse, a word about his life, family, future—none of this helps beyond the moment. He has no least idea of who we are, why we're locked in this iron jungle; not even the will to shrug his shoulders. Justice? Of justice there is none. He is taken from his cell to face more charges—stealing a ham, stealing a purse, a hopeless Fagin-child in the fist of the law.

For him—justice? His skin is his destiny. He is one of the kenneled souls under the altar, where the Lamb was sacrificed. How long, O Lord? The month or two we spend here, dishonored or forgotten or (worse) met with the quizzical frown, the politesse of academe and the Church—what a drop in the bucket of sweat, blood, suffering he is fated to endure.

May the cry of the heroic spirits be raised for him also: "How long, Oh Lord?"

"A terrible beauty is born." Transfigured humans stand by a sea of fiery glass. It is lit by their love, their courage. Their chant begins.

Lord God Almighty

The Lamb too is transfigured. He bears his wounds, a talisman of glory. No longer is he seen in a glass darkly. Now he too stands beside the sea of glory. All tempests calmed, the tides of human passion and conflict stilled. He is seen as he sees: Lord God Almighty. While he walked the earth, he was clothed in humiliation, an outcast, barely tolerated, marked like an offending tree with prophetic leaves, in the winds of God's justice—marked for destruction. He came audible to his own and they did not welcome him. But eternity is a moment of intolerable truth; those who bore witness to him in the days of his dishonor, live to honor him, and thereby themselves. They have become what he is, and forever. Is he now Lord? He was once servant, suffering servant in the words of Isaiah, verified in the decrees of Augustus Caesar, in his humiliated birth; verified by Herod and Pilate in his execution. The circle is forged. The dossier of Jesus Christ is closed. . . .

And yet—and yet, not quite, not by a long shot. The long shot is neither simple good luck, nor a last minute reprieve, nor a flicker of mercy in the eyes of authority, nor (before the fact) an act of God. No, he must go the whole way. "Put up your sword: do you not know, if I asked, the Father would send a legion of angels? It

is fitting to fulfill all justice.'' The justice of which he speaks raises that misused and harried word to a transcendent height. The justice to which he makes final appeal is the very eye and will of God. His cosmic order, the generations of sin and revolt and rebirth, the final righting of things whose form is known only to God. He casts himself into that sea, turbulent and bloody and choked with the debris of lost lives and shattered Utopias.

Now the sea has turned to glass. It is stilled by the hand of eternity. On its shore stand the twice born, saints, improbable and blinking in that light, genetic miracles out of the womb of time. "Lord God Almighty,'' they chant. We can perhaps now and again borrow such words, in fear and trembling, a daring seizure of eternity, a theft of fire. But only if we go the way they have gone, through "great tribulation"—"those who have not borne the mark of the beast'' who have not "worshipped him or followed after,'' those unseduced by his "great miracles.''

We had best tread easy here. Most of us find ourselves willy nilly, for most of our lives, gingerly treading a middle ground, buying off the beast, cajoling him, pacifying him, dickering with him. Most of us are post-Christians. Who of us has known a martyr, or indeed a fervent or heroic Christian in our circle of parish or work or home life? Who has carried into public places the word of God, heard or pondered in times of worship? We worship at a cold hearth. The burning coal that touched the lips of Isaiah has not purified us. So the astounding, weighty, majestic words of prayer are uttered as unfeelingly as a grocery list. The words are "wandering stars,'' idle arrows without a mark.

Today anyone can worship, anyone can invoke God (and does), anyone can be a Christian. Any Christian can take any job

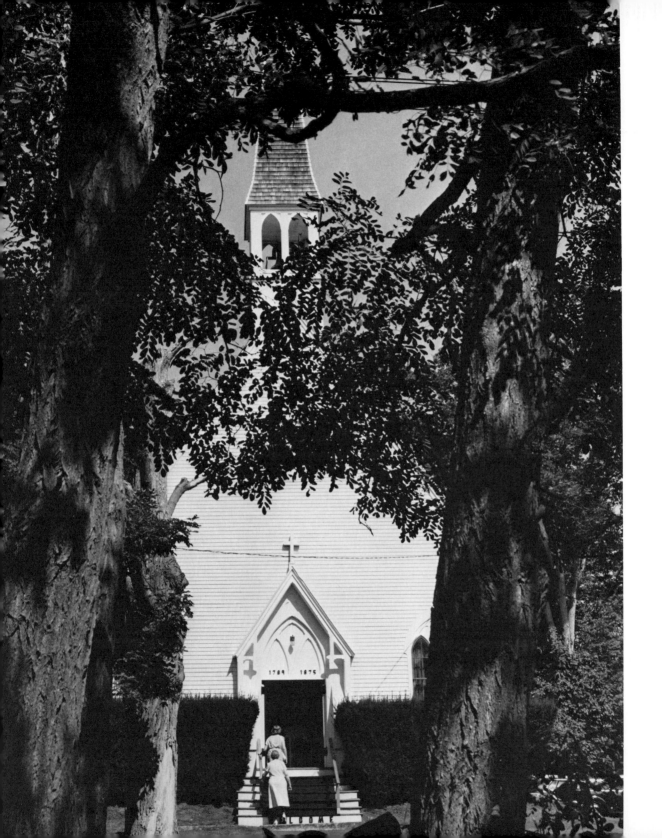

(presuming it is exalted enough to place its immorality beyond question.) Anyone can pass quietly from criminal deception, weapons production, illegal surveillance, laundering of money, disruption of legal dissent, and on to Sunday Worship—all with the unblushing conscience of the saved. Thus is religion ground into the belly of the Beast—a nourishing menu indeed.

And in lesser ways, who of us does not make a mockery of the Lord, the omnipotent one? A sort of willed impotence afflicts us; we walk into a moral quagmire, pay taxes for war, send our sons, brothers, lovers off to die or kill in the latest imperial adventure—more times than not with the blessing of our religious leaders, who have a notoriously clear eye when properties and exemptions are in question.

Who of us indeed can open our Bibles and read, simply and lucidly, what is written there? "Love your enemies. Do good to those who persecute you. If an enemy strike you in the face, turn the other cheek. . . Feed the hungry, clothe the naked." It is the charter of a reborn people. The words, enacted, believed, embraced in action, entitle us to turn with all our heart in the direction of the Lord.

Alas, our nation has long ago inducted us Christians. We have swelled the enthusiastic legions marching against the Vietnamese, Koreans, Germans, Japanese, Guatemalans. We have torn up our charter of the kingdom: it lies at our feet, the debris of God's promise, "A holy people, a priestly nation." And this year, Vietnam's blood-stained lesson unlearned, we heap up an unspeakable cache of nuclear weapons, designed for one purpose, a "first strike capability" against the earth and its peoples. Not merely do we preempt the last day of creation, we actually declare that our omnipotent Lord is, in brute fact, the war-making State. . . .

The prayer of the martyrs ought to be outlawed, forbidden on our lips. In the middle ages, popes placed whole towns under interdict. No public prayer, no eucharist, no baptisms, no burial service for the dead—until public crime was expiated. The Church could not continue the work of Christ while the will of Christ was violated, despised. In somewhat the same way today, the pope should order all churches closed, all services suspended in those nations which prepare nuclear war. A universal inderdict! For the nuclear arms race threatens the greatest crime since the crucifixion—the Hiroshimizing of all the earth, a firestorm, the finis of the human adventure. Experts predict that in ten years some thirty-eight nations will possess the bomb and the chances of nuclear war will thus increase immeasurably. And where are we? And where are we?

The moral void precedes the cosmic one, and prepares for it. Paul wrote to the early Church, warning that "the unholy one" would enter the temple, enthrone itself and declare itself God.

Are our lives a tribute to the true God? How many of us "follow after the beast," follow him even into the sanctuary, bow to him in that place, by silence, subservience, fervent consumerism, racism, lust for property and pride of place?

No one stands by the sea of eternity, the prayer "Omnipotent Lord God" on his or her lips, who has not passed through the fires.

In the very sanctuary, the Beast mouths his "blasphemies." He curses God, wishes him destroyed, wants no part with him, wants in fact, like a vile pied piper, to lead the faithful into his own "abyss."

He wishes us to turn, not to God, as our loving and powerful opposite. No—to himself.

[50]

His instrument is the Bomb. If he can dream it, create it, sell it, explode it! Then in all truth he will have dreamed us up, created us, sold us out, exploded our very existence. Then we become not the twice born, who are the dream of God, but the twice dead, those who fall victim to the "second death!"

Let us be quite clear. We cannot serve two masters. It is intolerable that American Christians, by some psychic sleight of hand, pay tribute to the Beast on the one hand and to the God of life on the other. We cannot serve God and the Bomb. We will despise the one and revere the other; the human spirit splits like a struck log in the impossible cross-grained service of life and death.

For several years, my friends and I have tried to serve the God of life by resisting the Unholy One in the Holy place. We believe the Bomb should not dwell there, enthroned. This is why I write these words from jail, in whatever urgency and clarity such a place awakens. We cannot live at peace with a false peace. Can our fellow Christians?

How Great and Wonderful Are Your Deeds!

The deeds of God.

Creation itself. Ourselves. The quick and the dead, the unborn. The martyrs above all, his temple, those who pray such words of praise with a heart of fire, a tongue of crystal; they are his triumph, eternity their booty, his face their reward. Can we see ourselves in their company?

In them, struggle has yielded to ecstasy. Resistance to the authority that destroyed them is ended; praise of God is the outcome, the other side of struggle. That other side is movingly described in

the letter to the Hebrews, where the faith of the saints is traced throughout its blood-stained history. That history is our own, as the letter insists:

The world was not good enough for them! They wandered like refugees in the deserts and hills, living in caves and holes in the ground. What a record all of these have won by their faith! . . . As for us, we have this large crowd of witnesses around us. Let us rid ourselves, then, of everything that gets in the way, and the sin which holds us captive, and let us run with determination the race that lies before us. Let us keep our eyes fixed on Jesus, on whom our faith depends from beginning to end.

(Heb. 11:38-12:2)

The praise of the martyr also has its "other side." What could be more contemptuous of the God of creation than the presence of the Beast in the sanctuary? We easily conclude that the wicked enthronement could never become part of our liturgy. No, it must belong to that dark other altar of communism. We overreach ourselves, we are blinded by our history of practiced contempt for God. Are our bombs pure, and the communists' impure? Or have we a mandate from God to build virtuous bombs, blessed perhaps by the sign of the cross, designed to clear the earth finally of all evildoers? Perhaps we picture our Lord buckling on his military armor, descending purposefully into the nuclear bunker, calmly pressing the button that splinters the world and burns humans to a bloody dust? Then perhaps (however briefly, until *they* push the button in retaliation against their "bad guys") we (and our Christ) could wash our hands clean in the same "bowl of God's anger." Then too, possibly, "our Christ" would turn to us; perhaps in our eager ears would sound, before he even spoke, the sweet anticipated military blessing, in the immoral words of every bloody commander in history, for a "job well done?" And finally what if this Christ of ours were to raise his visor, were to show us, not the gentle strength of the man of Nazareth—but the face of the Beast! And what if, as he stalked about to decorate his peerless troops, each of us, meeting that face, were to see there, as in a merciless mirror, our own face? The face of the Beast?

What then of our deeds—which we had presumed were the "great and wonderful deeds of God Himself?"

And who were we following, all those years (all those centuries) of blood and guts and crusades and crosses and *Te Deums?*

"Every time a bomb falls in Vietnam," wrote a Catholic from Saigon in 1966, "every time a village is burned or a child maimed, all your fine Christian words, your words about peaceable Christian intentions and good faith, are put to naught." Indeed. Most of us, I confess (my confession begins in my own house) most of us would not recognize a "deed of God" if it struck us head-on, fore or aft. Are we apt to confuse his deeds with our own? Commonly, it seems to me, we think of his deeds in moods which ring the cracked changes, from self-congratulation to anger to vague discontent (the mood range of spoiled children in a polluted playground)—we think of his deeds as the fretful stroking of a cosmic daddy on his feverish favorite offspring. By the dawn's early light, by the rocket's red glare, from shore to shining shore, he "keeps America beautiful"; it is "his country right or wrong." His works are truly great and wondrous: they range from the Rockefeller holdings, through

Exxon and Gulf and G.E. and Electric Boat and Sikorski and Boeing. He has an eye to the main chance; property is his politics, the police his Blue Army, the CIA the apple of his eye. His values, his cosmic plan, are no other than our own; only purified, elevated to the nth degree, pained no doubt at times, correcting a rough edge here, a contretemps there, reproving, conniving, collaborating, concluding various covenants atop Mt. Shasta. Our God, his people. His words, our responsibility. Was there ever in history a neater dovetailing of divine and human excellence? We are in awe—of ourselves.

No. His works are otherwise.

Let us think of them for a moment. As his word speaks of them, as those men and women praise them, who have first done those works, have passed through these fires.

——His works are performed in the desert, where people are at the end of their rope, without armies, weapons, protection, money, self-assurance, magic rites, strange gods.

——His works are a liberation. They unmask our inward slavery, our fitful wills, our egos, our violence.

——His works are penitential. They include a willingness on our part to endure his absence, his silence, his furious anger. They will not allow us our fifty-fifty compromise; so much for Caesar, so much for God. (For those who serve God, there is nothing left for Caesar.)

——His works are gracious, in the root sense of the word. His favor does not wait upon our "ups" and "downs," the narcotic of our moods, nudged this way and that by the tides of this world. "Turn to us that we may turn to you." His is the first move. Indeed how else could we be moved? A faith that moves mountains? Our

inertia and selfishness make very Himalayas of us.

——His works are peaceable. In this, alone, he is an utter stranger to our civilization. More, he is an outcast. We have loosed the hounds of war on the world, again and again—not in his name, as we fondly think—in the name of our own profound moral disarray, our racism, our hatred of his brothers and sisters, our self-hatred, finally. Finally! The ominous word is like the baying of the nuclear hell-hounds we hold on an uneasy leash. In the name of God, we do not flinch at slipping their collars. They will ravage the world.

——His works are modest. At times this seems to me the clue to his heart, the heart of Jesus, which bears a human shape and size. "Can any of you, by taking thought, add an inch to your stature?" "Work while it is day, for the night comes, when no one may work." "When you have done everything enjoined on you, say to yourself: we are profitless servants!" The words speak of a modesty which created the world to a human measure, which salvaged us, not by the spectacular onrush of legions of angels, but quite simply and directly—"laying down his life for his friends." And then the measure is set: "greater love than this no one may have!"

——And yet, his deeds are "great and wonderful." We know those works for what they are, only if we penetrate their spirit, undergo their testing. The point bears repeating. Its opposite is not the arrival of Superhuman; it is the abyss, the subhuman. The stolen fire consumes the thief. In the old Greek myth, the "hero" is punished in chains, a bird of prey eats at his vitals. A dreadful parable of the fate of modern war makers and those who bear the mark of the Beast. Envy eats them alive, they are self-consumed. Envy allows them no joy in their larcenous prize; every new weapon begets a new weapon, generation upon generation. The vulture that consumes them is the final consumer: cosmic envy, of one another. Of God Himself.

"Your deeds are great and wonderful." The broad scope of the Bible tells of them: creation, exodus, flood, promised land. Then Jesus, THE work of God. Great and wonderful indeed. . . .

And here in jail, the works shine out. Being a prisoner among prisoners has its rueful advantage; they know we are priests, that leads to questions; then we share our books, letters, cigarettes. Talk goes on. . . . One of the most damaged among them is a Vietnam veteran. His arm is stitched together like a rag doll's. His mouth runs on compulsively, day and night. But at least, I say to myself, we've turned a corner here, religion might show a different face. . . . And I think of that promise, almost a tease, of the Lord: "If you believe, you will do greater works than I have done." Greater than he? Either we do not believe, which would account for the ashen tastes in our mouths, the handfuls of ashes (our "works") we carry witlessly about; or we do believe (at least long to believe, at least are desperately conscious of not believing worth a damn), and then our works surprise our eyesight, our arm's measure and outreach. Ultimately, I suppose we leave it all to Another, a kind of curtain raiser on death. A letting go. And with good heart.

——And, finally, I think his works are imaginative. And for this I thank him most of all. Who else but God could imagine Jesus, Mary, the saints? And John tells us—it was in and through him that God imagined the world. The whole sorry, trivial, blood-shot, messy, furious, equivocal, unthinkable marvel. Created it, took it all into account, suffered for it! And won through. Not a still life, but a tragic drama, a wrestling match between a free and skillful human and a sweating, desperate slave. Who could have imagined it, before the fact? . . . In jail, the least start and tic of goodness, life, hope, awakens this sense.

Or one pauses ruefully in his tracks—who would ever have imagined, in the strait-laced days of my youth, that I would be cast in here? Delicious, ironic! One imagines in jail, by way of deprivation, the juicy, various world "outside." The surf off Block Island, the tattered, dusty stretches of Riverside Park in midsummer, a hero sandwich of races and tongues and games and princes and dogs and children and idlers and snoozers and jugglers and beggars. Broadway and 98th, huggermugger of noise, commerce, cheap goods and disservices, faces and fruits, the outspread potlatch of the tribes of earth! Like Ulysses, I cry in wonder; the places I have traveled, the sights my eyes have seen!

And more. The One who imagined the visible things of this world, imagined also the invisible. And Paul consoles us: set your eyes, not on the things which are seen, but on the unseen. . . . The sun creeps along the bars' length, a living hourglass, a sundial in a dead time. The voices of children, traffic, lace a moment of rare silence. The heart stops in its tracks, bemused by a grace beyond telling. Ecstasy, gratitude, a hint, a start. Between heartbeats we know our heart is in place—it beats on, out of sight, mostly out of mind, like the heart of the world. We are comforted and calmed— and can go on. . . .

Billy lies under his brown blanket in the corner bunk, like a heap of earth. Dust to dust. Stupefied, near dead. He heaves out like a blind prehuman to take his grub, stalk about for a while, and then dig in again. He has stopped living at twenty-two. Now and

again when we speak kindly to him, kid him, hand him a cigarette, his eyes come alive like a struck match. Soon quenched. Has God imagined this disaster? A blasphemy to think it. We are godlike to the degree we can imagine that "new heavens and new earth" he promises. To imagine is to create, to embody. God's world did not remain in his head. Neither can the new earth. Test your imaginings. What are you creating? What do you envision?

King of All Nations

What is this? The blessed ones, by the sea of eternity, voicing a political prayer? That word, *nations,* what a Pandora's box it opens!

The people of all nations, the holy ones, address the Lord— King of all nations! We are not to conjure up a knot of innocents, waving flags before a potentate. Not really.

They so address him because they have surpassed nationhood—that furious fiction that puts us all in square boxes and borders and jails and armies and death rows. "In Christ neither slave nor free, male nor female. For you are all one in him."

But now, nose to nose they stand, the hellhound nukes, Russian and American, a no-win impasse, and the transfixed peoples hiding out on earth, keeping a low profile before Armageddon— our energies drained, our hope all but dead. . . .

The nation invokes God and wheels out its weapons. CORRECTION: the nation wheels out its god and invokes its weapons. This is the truth of the matter.

But the just ones by the shore of eternity have refused to wor-

ship the image of the Beast. Their God is the true God. Their lips are clean.

For our sake, their prayer is political: it beseeches the common good of all by invoking Goodness itself.

We do well to note this.

We can evoke their prayer, make it our own, only if we too are guilty of the Great Refusal, in the eyes of the nation (the all-seeing eye of the Beast). A *no* to death precedes, gives weight to, a *yes* to life.

Guarded borders, national frenzies, stacked weapons reaching to high heaven—we carve the earth like a corpse, everyone's kingdom ends at his or her own "property," we mime our own death in our shrinking hegemony. Mine is not yours. I am not you. Property is politics. In the words of a recent Texan chief of state to an admiring nation, in the midst of the rape of Southeast Asia: "They want what we got. They aren't goin' to git it!" Indeed.

A collision course, for humanity itself. We cannot keep what we've got without murder. Stark as that.

Such sentiments, willy-nilly, lay bare the marrow bones of the Church as well as the State. The imperial State drags religion along behind its chariot, a corpse mutilated beyond recognition. It comes to this: modern war, the invention and horrid game of the Christian West, drags the dead Church in its wake, its talisman, its bloody good-luck charm.

Or a modern image occurs. In the opening sequence of the Italian film *La Dolce Vita,* a colossal statue of Christ is airborne over Rome, dangling from cables below a helicopter, to be lowered on the spire of a new church. The city roars below, indifferent to the bizarre burden. The statue, a frozen parody of the Second Com-

ing, dangles from the chopper; a cold eye, a blessing forever futile, static. Whatever. Whatever. No matter what crime or folly, an indiscriminate blessing, bestowed by a dead image borne aloft, dead weight and all, by the roaring locust. Technology is in charge, it will lower the *deus ex machina* where and when it chooses, will work such marvels at its own whim. And the multitudes marvel, not that the lord of history has "returned on clouds of glory," but that the Beast has verified *his* promise—the seduction of the nations: "All the earth followed after the Beast." Christ has lost his capital letter. The Beast has gained one.

Jail is a good place to say that prayer: *Lord of all nations*. The nation has put us here. Our plea is on behalf of life, an indictable offense. We plead against universal ruin, already well underway. The people live at peace with war. The people pay for war—and the people, their human needs, are swept aside, mere debris in the chariot's wake. I live in a rotting neighborhood, in a city slowly falling to its knees. Our poor wear the look of debased chattel, inferior end products, reduced for quick sale. There is care neither for the aged, nor the infirm, nor children. People die in icy apartments, their bodies ravaged by hunger. Meantime the president addresses the nation in a "fireside chat" (the poor are perhaps warmed by an image of an open fire). He calls for austerity in energy use, heat, lights. And he fails with sublime oversight to mention that the military daily consume one third of all energy available to two hundred million people. Military "needs," a Gargantuan, slovenly appetite, lie beyond question. The fleets must prowl the seas, the great birds heave aloft with their doomsday cargoes. They are guarding the corpse of a land, the death of a hope.

When we pray, we pray to an exiled king, a renegade among the peoples, a ragtag holy one, steeped in dishonor. He is the sport and mockery of all, pushed to the edge of the world, edged out of consciousness. America, America, God shed His grace on thee. . . . "They have stolen my Lord away, and I do not know where they have hidden him."

Risen from the dead, certainly, but we live in a strange pause of time; time has stopped between one breath and the next, frozen. Can we savor that bitter moment of the Magdalen, which is the very coloration of life today? "Lord of the Nations." But he is dead and buried, level with the earth.

Grant us at least the presence of your absence. Let us taste that void, at the heart of the raucous yelling of prisoners, the void between the bars, between the hours that hang around like days, the days that stand like years. Touch our hearts that die in your absence. Bitter, bitter.

How Right and True Are Your Ways!

You have said: I am the way.

But here we are on ice. Do your ways lead to a dead end, a stalemate? "How right and true your ways. . ."

Your ways began in your mother's body. A journey ordered by Caesar. You were in his clutch from the beginning. "A decree went out from Caesar Augustus that all citizens register themselves for the census. . . . Everyone traveled to his own town to register." They were shunted about, driven onto the open roads, as the poor invariably are. And later, forced to flee a pogrom, into Egypt; a whey-faced, local pretender sought the life of this mysterious babe who haunted his nightmares.

What strikes one is the crashing stereotype of imperial method. Number the people. Everyone is a potential cannon plug, a work-horse, or a source of revenue. The poor are historically necessary. They make bricks without straw. They pay tithes of their sweat, until a war is declared, and a ruddier tribute is demanded. They build pyramids to house the "immortal longings" of dream-ridden fanatics. Powerful ones, how wrong, how treacherous are your ways.

Submit. We submit. In small ways, a modesty that cuts us down to size; only the modest may walk in his ways; those whose estimate of themselves is just, who are rightly contemptuous of infallible programs, five-year plans, sucking up to the powerful.

Your ways. Not a mere road map, directions from on high, the earth mover moving all before it.

A way which is a life. His life is us. A way that can never be the world's way. That way of the world, which is brutal, treach-erous, and finally, circular. A closed circle. A circle of hell, a point of no return.

And then—his way. Which he walked, literally as well as in principle. The good teacher never recommending a way he has not first of all walked. He went, as they say, "all the way." Then, mysteriously risen from the dead, he joins the two disheartened friends on the road. They are attempting, so to speak, to "undo the way" they have walked—"And we once believed that it was he who was to liberate Israel." They are filled with unhealed regret, the anguish of a lost cause. What is to be done when the way has

failed, and the way ahead looks only slightly more bleak than the way behind? What is to be done? He walks with them. He goes their way. He opened the scripture. "How dull, how slow to believe. Was not the messiah bound to suffer all this, before entering his glory?"

It was no thunderbolt struck them on that spring morning. It was like a slow healing. Like the blind man, they saw nothing; then they saw "trees like people moving"; then they quite simply saw. It was because his ways were slowly becoming their own; their minds were unclogging; they were beginning to see, even as they were seen. Because THE way walked graciously with them.

His way—of seeing the world. How far we have gone afield, in a maze, a labyrinth of hell. We need no scripture to threaten us— we already dwell in the pit. (One feels at times like pausing on a busy street, turning to someone, anyone, saying, sweetly: "Pardon me, do you realize that we are the dead, that we are lock, stock and barrel, in hell?" They would crucify you.)

Still, we have traveled ways which are not his ways . . . and have already arrived, the dead at a dead end. That is why, in nature as well as in our foreboding minds, the words of scripture apply; perturbations, a vast range of catastrophes, mindless human shifts in the night, people dislodged from a spiritual center, magicians and fakirs hustling their wares. And above and beyond all this, the very meaning of the sacred aped, derided, parodied, like the obscene rites on the altar of Notre Dame Cathedral at the height of the French revolution. The Beast enters the holy place and enthrones itself there.

What then are "his ways" which the holy ones extol as right and true? We do well (Paul) to keep our eyes "fixed on Jesus, author and exemplar of our faith." I think the hardest thing is still the simplest thing. "Love one another as I have loved you." I do not know when we will come upon a better way, a more intent savior.

Yet Christian Americans, along with others, are afflicted with the quartan fever: every four years a new savior appears in the heavens! He spruces up the old discredited myth, proclaims a right and true way. No matter that he nudges aside an older one who promised exactly the same harnessing of nebulae: new frontiers, new society, peace with honor. No matter that he rules a decaying kingdom, rotting cities, despoiled countryside, that he speaks inevitably for the corporate powers who have put him in nomination. Memories are short; consciences bent; his "image" is good. Does not the prayer take a healthy, skeptical look at all this jabberwocky? The holy ones who chant this prayer have never bowed the knee before the imperial demand. Safe to say, quite simply: they never paid a tax inscribed "death." They never mis-served in the military dis-service. Conversion to Christ meant simply that one laid down arms: an expression with a delicious double sense, i.e., one refused to be the enemy of official State enemies and one made peace up close, where one lived—peace with family, friends, strangers, children, animals, the inoffensive earth. One was a friend of the earth.

Blessed are the peacemakers. This meant that one had to dig deep. There were few or no cultural reasons to nudge one into such a startling "way"; one needed a tradition deeper than this or that civilized spasm; life was not, after all, a matter of impulse, of moving beads along a string on an abacus, totting up gains and losses. No, it was a matter of a human style, of winning others by the evidence of a life lived intensely, at peak, graciously, modestly— dare I say poetically—for others.

[72]

Show us your ways. Ours are at a dead end, a cul-de-sac.

To survive in America, you need something more than America. Your ways?

To survive as a Christian in America, you need something better than Christianity, as commonly presented in America. Your ways.

It is not a matter of an "international style" (whatever that is). Catholics have invoked that shibboleth before. Today it has the sound of a cracked trumpet. The fact is, here, there and everywhere, acculturated religion (roughly defined as paganism after a sheep-dip) is languishing, on its way downhill. Sundown is upon us, the sheep are disconsolate. And the sheepfold is a ruin. (What a, pardon me, lousy metaphor in any case, for the twice-born sons and daughters of absolute fire!)

Your ways, how right and true!

The lips of the holy ones are touched by the fiery coal seized from the altar. They speak the language of the dead who are living. They invoke the ways of the One who is God, not of the dead, but of the living.

It is the "nations" who must someday echo this neglected, despised prayer. This is a point we miss. Do we miss it because we want to? We have known only a few (primitive) forms of uniting human life: Christendom, the nation state. Both have been a disaster. The second, the nation state, perhaps a final one.

In pondering this text, I think of an American president kneeling under the cameras in some religious shrine. (Such a scene, as a matter of fact, occurs all the time.) Trouble is, such a scene is so shot through with chauvinism, self-satisfaction, cozying up to some purported god-on-our-side militarism (we won again) as to be in no sense an authentic biblical sign. Rather it must be considered a remarkable example of idolatry—the nation divided between admiration for itself and veneration of the god of social violence.

If the nations are to worship in truth the God of nations, the nations must resign their nationhood; which is to say, exploitative sovereignty, domestic injustice, racism, military structures, diplomatic duplicity, multinational ripoffs, FBI voyeurism. They must be exorcised of the myths their rulers live by; a truly Orwellian nightmare where lies are truth, virtue is purely a domestic growth, and the crimes of authority are simply invisible. . . .

Meantime, of course, we live in a raw cold twilight—a mean time. A jungle of wrong questions infests the minds of leaders and citizens alike. Shall we dare destroy a single nuclear warhead (we have thousands to choose from) by way of "signal" to our implacable enemies? Shall we shave one or two billions from a military budget, a gesture roughly equivalent to surgery on the pimple on the derrière of a rogue elephant?

The paths of the Lord are not our paths.

It seems to me that sitting in jail is an exercise in both lunacy and savvy. In a sense, a mix of both, not easily separated out as to ingredients. I'm here because I was following "his ways"—so I firmly believe. And that conviction renders the whole mechanism of punishment or rehabilitation redundant.

Punishment for what? Rehabilitation to what? The *what*s are of a pressing nature. The loony bin; this place is composed of roughly equals parts of boredom, pinching of space, suspension in time, nose rubbing with strangers whose vision of the good life is not precisely one's own. The way of the Lord leads to a concrete bunker set flush in a dead end. No where to go—for a while, at least. What a way!

I never thought of such a way! I was a fairly stereotypical

[75]

young man, "tracked" as they say these days—to the way of the American Jesuits; a heavy dose of obedience, go here, come there. We were waited on, our future was as sheltered as our present, we were instant triumphs of an old-time religion, cozy as mechanical birds in a Swiss cuckoo clock. The roof was tight, the hours struck right. A nest of folklore for nestlings, teachable, docile, mostly attentive. How secure were your ways!

Your ways—or our investments?

Then, as of this morning, it all ended, here. In an old jail among minor low lives and losers. No big deal, thirty days going nowhere. Except that symbolically, as the life and self-understanding of the Order is concerned, the reverberations are bound to be intense. Are we not the apple of the eye of America? Does not every eye turn one way (not merely Catholic eyes at that) when the Jesuit myth marches by?

The center will not hold. The myth falls apart.

In some way that all but escapes the mind, a simple act like our protest at the Pentagon, flares like a signal in the night. His ways are other than our ways. The institutions have seized the souls of all and captivated them. We have played patsy with the bully boys in the back rooms (and front parlors) of power, money, dramatized ego. Let us then put aside our superman suits, our clerical greasepaint, and look level in the mirror—perhaps our faces are as bullying as the biggest "benefactor" we know. In any case, are not our bodies only the slimmest of evidence for a "vow of poverty"?

Good and bad, inextricably mixed—when I think of the intent and style of this action, or of my life itself. In any case, I have utterly failed with authorities; that is a cool fact, apart from any feeling I may have about it (I have the deepest feeling). I have had to go beyond, to strike out on my own. His ways, as I hope. . . . And this, to indulge in the understatement of the century, has not been well received. But at some point, about ten years ago, a question put itself to my soul, without trouble or anguish (though there had been plenty of both, long before): Was I to follow the old way, of consultation, dependence, delay, filtering my conscience through five or ten coolers—or was I to seek different counselors, in effect, a different way?

I went what is sometimes called, as an example of Perdition's Process, "my own way."

I too, of course, have a contention. (No Jesuit of whatever persuasion or color would be caught dead without one.) It went roughly like this: in order to be faithful to the gospel way (beyond doubt our first conscientious burden as Christians) it was of import, in such a hideous pressing event as the Vietnam War, to issue, loudly, clearly, declamatorily, peremptorily, one's soul's cry NO. One was required further to search out others afflicted with equal horror and loathing, in order to swell the chorus. If Jesuits would join that chorus, all to the good: we would perhaps be redeeming our souls and vindicating our existence. If Jesuits would not stand and speak, one must go elsewhere, seek another fraternity for life.

By and large the Jesuits would not speak. Therein lies a story too complex for these pages. But they would not. We, to put the matter crudely, had not after all been bombed. Word of the war was received by Jesuit academics as it was received generally by academics of whatever stripe or competence. A quizzical, tweed-laced frown, a drumming of the fingertips, that faint hint of civilized exasperation which is more damning than a fishwife's abuse. I was not an expert, and they were—in economics, political science, phi-

losophy, scripture even. Expertise (horrid word, horrid reality) bred acedia, contempt, a labyrinthine complication of mind. . . . Besides, like all of us, these fine spirits had been forged in the hot and cold furnace of three or four wars, invasions of foreign shores, McCarthy (one of us, after all). In my bailiwick, moreover, through the gates of Fordham trundled on great occasion the mandarin form of Cardinal Spellman: *cui servire regnare est*. They named a building after him; at his nod, third-rate tyrants from Latin American or Southeast Asia were accorded the honors of the campus, conferred by the genius of the place, a whip-tongued Irishman.

The world. Your ways, your ways! What it all means, this jail, the Jesuits, barnstorming around the country, teaching, writing—I would be the most arrant of fools to try to say. To justify myself. To construct a "case" for the defense. No, these are not salutary projects for such days as these (for any days?).

Who Will Not Fear You, Lord?

To put the answer shortly, Christians won't.

Indeed, in this matter of fear Christians yield to no one in their "correct attitude"—what might be called the hallmark of impeccable citizenship. We fear what everyone else fears: recession of the magic dollar, decline of neighborhoods, loss of job, ill health, the arrival of "them" next door. And of course, death. Not, it goes without saying, sins of injustice, crimes of the military, plagues of torture and repression, the rip-off of resources of the world, the deaths of children. . . .

Not, usually—God and his judgments.

The phrase has an ominous, a faintly anachronistic ring. Are we then to propitiate this God in some mad dance of death, awaken a prehuman sense of guilts long done with? Absurd!

Strange on the other hand, how the blessed ones who chant this prayer, announce the fear of God as a foregone conclusion. The implication goes something like this: Who would be so foolish, would so play hob with reality, would stand so far aside from right order—as not to fear you?

Note too, please, how the direct address ("you") also fore-closes the insanity of any other course than the "fear of the Lord." If God is a "you," beyond any doubt he is present. He is the opposite number of those who pray; he is the listener; but those who refuse the prayer, refuse the fear, are outside this mysterious converse. They are a mere "it," not even a third party to what can only be seen as an exchange of love. They stand outside the light. They cannot even be described as silent witnesses to the converse; no, they have declared themselves; consigned themselves to a place the old fashioned have a word for.

There are not many human analogues, I think, for this "fear" I am trying to understand. Is it news to anyone that we are enduring a time of massive human breakup? I think it is not. We are bewil-dered, overwhelmed at times, by a sense of our own helplessness, as we watch human lives, individuals, marriages, friendships break-ing apart like damp earth turned over by a plowshare. Whose hand on the plow? We do not know—the hand may as well be holding a sword. Nothing, literally nothing, holds. Neither good intentions nor fervent vows, nor the marriage-mucilage of children.

The point of all this is not merely a pointless threnody.

It is this: we have very few viable images of the mystery of fear of God. This fear, an intuitive sense of respect for the presence

of another, a loved one hearkened to, an adversary who calls shots on my faults, one who sets me going in directions I would not have taken. Life is gracious and full when I can rejoice in two or three such friends (one such lover). Life is empty, boring, deadly colorless, hardly life at all, when I stand in it, alone, the very epitome, the empty husk of the sorrowful, alienated, anxiety-ridden post-Christian. Such a one is even incapable of the fear we speak of. Too afraid, in short, to embrace the fear of the Lord. Too locked in.

"Who will not fear the Lord?" An attitude of creatureliness. We are called to be Godlike—in our very refusal to play God! Is not this the rub? According to the Bible, the economic and military sharks of the empire are the working parts of the empire itself. Working in concert, they create structures that amount to a massive worldwide nightmare, animated by "a Beast," enticing, aggrandizing, deceiving, alienating, working all kinds of violence, exploiting, sucking the earth dry, corrupting language, creating psychological and spiritual havoc, making casualties of strong and virtuous wills, enlisting all other structures (including the Church itself) into a stupendous network of "goods and services." This, in fine, is the Beast which is to be feared. "The whole world followed after. . . . He was allowed to perform great miracles. . . . They cried 'Who is like the Beast? Who can prevail against him?' "

The monstrous parody is in full sway.

Who would not fear you, the Beast?

The displacement of modern consciousness; radically, away from reality. We fear that which sane minds would despise. We despise the One whom the truth of reality would lead us to fear. . . .

I write this, sitting before a hefty set of bars, denizen of a cage

constructed to constrain (contain, tame) outlandish spirits. Can I
say to my soul (peace!) that I am here solely because I fear the
Lord and because I have no fear of the Beast? Is that my offense?

According to my prophetic namesake, the Beast, having staked
his claim in the world (a fairly uncomplicated task), comes prowling
around the sanctuary. It is at this point that he takes on a totally
different character. This is his first risky foray into unknown ter-
ritory. The hair rises along his spine, his lethal eyes sharpen. He
leans forward to the spoor of the divine; like a negative charge of
energy, he seeks his opposite number: how shall he be himself, the
adversary, the anti-, until he encounters Christ? He is on the outer
porch, a dark stain moving along the pavement; he lumbers upright,
pulls the great ring of the portal, falls forward, inside! Up the aisle
the Unmentionable shuffles, the nameless, the number, the con-
catenation of horrors, "the abominable thing that causes desola-
tion." He reaches the altar, hops up, dislodging the golden
instruments, fouling the linens. Squats there blinking. He locks and
unlocks his jaws—arrived!

Now the issue is joined. . . .

The trouble with the fundamentalists is—they're so nearly right
it hurts. They have a warier eye for the Beast, even the Beast in
Sunday clothes, than the groomed liberal, cushioned from reality
all week, resigned and passive on his worshipful Sabbath pew! The
Beast? nonsense . . . merely an unexpected outsider, a bit bizarre
of course, probably only passing through. Good fellowship, sir! Join
us for after service coffee, do! His manicured hand! It trembles as
he grasps that not quite human hand.

The lack of fear is appalling—having no fear of the Beast, how
shall we fear the Lord?

Finally, I come back to the place I've never left these twenty-three days—this adamantine womb.

The fear of jail. Most people cannot imagine being here. Even in such a time as ours, confronted, as we all are, by a common prospect—that of adding with our sweet flesh and tender bones to the ash heap of creation. But that is no "prospect," in the sense of a vivid possibility, a vision of horror that energizes. It numbs, chills, like gradual death before a wintry dawn. No galvanic response, not even a muscular tic.

So the conscience dies, in face of a terror too great to encompass. I cannot imagine the death of everyone; I cannot even imagine, in any real way, my own death. Which is to say, not that my phantasy fails me as to hour, moment, circumstance, that I have no vivid image of how to die well. Conscience stops short, the screen is blank, better, it is burnt out.

Can I imagine then how to live well? Probably not, since the image, if it existed, would include both acts—the continuum: living-dying well.

I think fear is the outpost which signals "danger" to the conscience, keeps it fuzzy at the edges of experience, finally reduces us to time's robots. All the human parts are there, but they move on a narrow track. Beyond is only—the beyond.

Which ought not to be, to say the least.

Fear of jail, fear of death: the opposite of fear of the Lord. The first is an incantation, a tribute paid to death itself. It conjures up all sorts of vague horrors: extinction, torment, the void. It cannot push them back, these phantasmagoria (always larger than life, arrogant surrogates of reality), or pierce their inflation, or bring them down to size.

Fear of the Lord always shows itself, biblically, in a genetic, even an ironic way. It implies that one stands before one other; one for, and against one other; the friend who fears the friend, the lover the lover. Such fear is charged with ironies, contradictions that repulse like a living force, affinities that startle and delight, hatreds, hopes.

If I fear you, how can I love you? The question is incorrectly put. More exactly, if I love you, how can I not fear you?

The Bomb is a very tower of Babel dedicated to the proposition that the builders need fear neither God nor humans. And it is no sooner built, armed, calibrated, poised, incanted, praised, stroked, polished, checked, guarded, reverenced, than we discover a whole new galaxy of fear! We fear that another nation may also have the Bomb, its god, its IT; half an inch taller, a quarter inch fatter, one-sixteenth inch more accurate, one-thirty-second inch more lethal. . . . Now we must fear, with thousands of such doomsday toys scattered about the devilish nursery, must fear, not just one opposite number, but thirty or forty. Like multiple reflecting mirrors, they show back at us, and we at them, and all of us at one another, a perfect, cold, static image of fear; a stalemate in the root sense of the word ("mates" in the game of death, "stale" images of mutual death). He who grabs the sword starts an infinite series of such mirror images—creates his opposite number in the very act of violence ("opposite" in the sense of cold will to destroy the other; "number" in a sense we know too well after Vietnam, the body count, the hunter's vile competition).

We fear those who have the Bomb, their IT.

We fear those who may be, or actually are, in the process of creating their own IT.

In such a world, the You, the Other, the Beloved, has no place.

In such a world, the fear of the Lord, a virtue stemming from moral sanity, genetic connections, equality and dignity and conquest of violence— all this goes up the flue. It is the smoke of the death of a great hope, moral attainment.

This sense of God, this liberating fear, is lost; it is like the Ming ceramic technique or the glass blowing of Chartres windows. We shall have to seek this fear in places as wild and distant as Cathay. Among certain despised, poor, outcast peoples, worshipping in odd corners of the mad earth; in them the sense of God persists. And finally, in that "little flock" who raise their song by the sea of glass. Do they seem remote from us? Indeed they are, their song is as foreign as the inhuman whine and clatter of our weaponry is familiar. Bow down before the omnipotent IT; fear only IT.

Let us, now and then, do ourselves a favor. For sweet sanity's sake, close our eyes, stretch out our arms. Dwell for a few moments in a world which is the real world, but which, because of the seizure of that world by demons of technique, can for the present only be imagined. Not in the sense, certainly, of vain phantasy; but in the sense that (name your country) such a world is variously derided, outlawed, forbidden. No less real for its interdiction, perhaps more real for that. In the sense that it is marked by the blood and tears of those who "stand by the sea of glass" and by all their sisters and brothers who believe and struggle on in the world.

Imagine such a world! It is populated, not by Titans and mad competitors, but by a creaturely and modest community. It is a world in which the fear of the Lord is the human current that binds one to the other, hand to hand, man to woman, friend to friend, lover to lover. It is a world, it is a dance; its rhythm is the lively moving order of the universe itself. It circles about you, a friend, a lover.

Who Will Refuse to Declare Your Greatness?

In eternity (the scene of the prayer) the question is of course, sublimely redundant.

On earth, the question hangs on the air, still unanswered (therefore idly posed)—unanswered by the nations, by the Church, by the individual.

Must we not go further?

Unanswered? Worse than that. Answered in the negative. We will refuse!

The history of humankind, even after the coming of Christ, is a history of the great refusal. Therefore, there are martyrs.

Therefore, there are wars; the bombs which are the malevolent fruit of empire, its national harvest, commemorate the refusal. Why declare your greatness? Our greatness is greater than yours. We will build a tower reaching to high heaven.

We will concoct a being greater than you, an ominous god of death, a being greater than God. Our IT will suspend the promise, cancel the last day; better, It will preempt his second coming, strip HIM of all glory, confront him with "the work of our hands"— humanity erased, the sweet and living earth reduced to a smoking clinker.

The Church? The Church will no longer signify. Henceforth

our Bomb will declare the terms of so called "salvation." They will be saved who consent to worship the Bomb, the Frankenstein created by the Beast in his own image and likeness.

The Body of Christ? No more. The besotted adoring multitudes "following after the Beast," transform the genetic patterns of existence. men and women, coalescing mutely around the shrines of nuclear gods, are transformed into the Body of the Beast.

Eucharist? The rulers of the earth announce bread and circuses for the obedient. For the others, the disobedient, the witless who will not read the signs of the times, there are two outcomes. Put to death, all those who refuse to worship the Beast; and prevent from buying and selling all those who do not bear the mark of the Beast. Physical death, economic sanctions, the choices are not large.

The saints refuse the Great Refusal. Their crime: they raised the prayer: "Who will refuse to declare your greatness?" A question which the world will not tolerate. They raised the question. It was a capital offense, and they paid for it.

They raised the question, in the Church as well as in the world. Being themselves the Church, the Body of Christ, how could these holy ones refuse to praise God, to raise the question of resistance to the Beast, to raise it loud and clear and constant, day and night?

They raised the question in the Church for the sake of the world, that the world might be twice born, might die as the Great Refuser, and be reborn in the Body—which is the world's destiny. But not yet.

And they raised the question in the world for the sake of the Church. It was not enough, they sensed, to raise the question as a kind of cultish formula, to raise the question only during worship, in a church building (always a safe place) among those who nod in agreement, and sing in unison. Such Christians know full well that such praise, such a question, means exactly nothing. They know (they must know) that praise of God is an empty sham until one has refused the Beast—"awe, reverence, the bearing of its mark."

In churches, how can the question be a real question? No, the question is a worldly question, it must be raised in face of the principalities and powers, in the face of the Beast. It must be raised in the street, at the Pentagon, at the bunkers and test sites, in the laboratories where death is the pushbutton product, at the White House. In such places, the question takes on a bloody urgency. "The Beast was allowed to fight against God's people and to defeat them."

They were God's people, not because they flocked to temples, for empty worship, but because they raised the question of the "great refusal" in public, in the grandiose halls and very temple of the Beast.

They knew what the price would be. They were not simpletons or fanatics. They had a burning unrequited sense of justice; it outlasted the injustice of their condemnations. Even after death they cry out for requital, the righting of the wrongs that destroyed them. . . . How long, oh Lord?

Does not their question, raised in eternity, as a song of triumph, a song that affirms God (his greatness) as well as themselves—does it not retain the most vivid sense of time and this world? They have not won eternal life by wiping out the memory of the earth, of those who refused, of those who were heroic and patient and (by turns) outspoken, whose worship was the sacrifice of their bodies, whose prayer had ominous public consequences for themselves.

The prayer is charged with a weight of indignation, of judgment. Those who refuse are judged by those who perish.

"The Beast was allowed to wage war on the saints, and to defeat them."

How pleasant it would be to forget the bitter outcome of death. But if the Beast is the ape of immortality, what other outcome is possible for the saints?

We wish to raise the question.

We wish to join the question to responsible work in the world. We wish to raise the question before the Church.

We wish to raise the question, as a great cry of faith, in the Church for the sake of the world.

"The Beast was allowed to defeat the saints."

On the understanding of this, everything depends.

Not that, as they say, "life is a conflict," a truism everybody knows and runs with, in a hundred directions—heroes and knaves, torturers and victims, the powerful and the wretched. No, a statement that cuts nearer the bone, referring as it does, not just to anybody—the indeterminate mass of hot, cold and lukewarm— but to a precise conflict, a moral one, a matter of conscience. Those whose conscience is not a chaos or a grab bag or a miser's trove or a cesspool. A conflict between light and darkness, between the Beast and the holy ones.

The interests of the Beast center around the valiant. Can he defeat them, neutralize them, absorb them?

He cannot. The metaphor which describes them is intense, classical; they have not worn the mark of the Beast, not been intoxicated with the obscenities of the great whore.

But the Beast is the god of death. Capital punishment is his

final card. He wields it with a broad swath. War is his natural element, and the saints a "natural" enemy. His consummate war, the war which underlies all other wars, for which the history of war is a metaphor, a cover, is the war against the saints.

The news is—he wins.

The word falls like a trap door.

It is a word issuing not from the Beast, which would be natural enough. Every general relishes a good bloody win; we are all used to those communiqués, composed of equal parts of vanity and deceit, designed above all to dishearten the credulous, to keep minds teetering, off balance, as well as to feed national pride and consecrated violence.

But this word issues from God. The Beast does battle with the saints; he wins. . . .

Yesterday fourteen of us prisoners were transferred here. In chains. Under a shotgun-wielding servant of public weal, in a Black Maria notable neither for light nor ventilation. We were transported across town. (How many transports for Philip and myself!) Climbing into the van was a particularly clumsy maneuvre for fourteen men chained together. And the whole trip lay under the icy sign of death, double barreled. Entering the van, we had to snake around in a circle, half-stooped, trying to sort out hands and feet, right and left.)

The Beast wins. He is allowed to defeat the saints. I can offer no great insight into such a stupendous saying. But I am somewhat less ignorant of it than I was a day ago. . .

Kim Chi Ha, the Korean Christian, poet, prisoner, knows it well and bitterly. You inch forward in that knowledge, or you inch away from it. There are no fast trips, no short cuts. Though there

[95]

are detours aplenty, and deceiving signposts and cul-de-sacs. Age is no guarantee of attainment, nor youth, nor intelligence, nor prestige. (Not even the Jesuits can have this credential Xeroxed for their members.)

It is, in the quaint phrase, a matter of grace.

The Beast is allowed to defeat the saints.

So the vaunted, the greatest, the serpent, the Beast, the Deceiver, the Accuser, the Bomb, the Imperial State (it is all one), is hemmed in by a greater? Yes. He "is permitted" to do what he does.

This horrendous scene of the victory of evil, is hemmed in as by two great arms, a closure, a parenthesis of grace.

The nature of violence is essentially unlimited. But here a limit is declared.

A limit to defeat? To death itself?

Yes. He "was permitted" to defeat the saints.

At this point one feels like rising from the mad floor where I scrawl these notes (chairs are not among our amenities here) to chant a song of triumph. All praise to Jesus, in whom we overcome. Death, where is your victory, where is your sting?

The Beast may defeat the valiant ones, but he can hardly claim a victory. His immortality is spurious; it signifies merely an apish mime of the resurrection of Christ, no more than the persistence of ego, exploitation, the violence of the structures of the world. Hypostasized no doubt, infesting, granted certain times and places in which to function, granted even, all times and places, wherever clots of power converge into the cancerous organism called empire.

Still, limited. We have his word for it. Indeed, death which is a condign weapon of the Beast, is inverted by the act of God; it becomes a gateway to victory.

[96]

You Alone Are Holy

This is a word one would almost wish to pass by. Who are we to speak such words? We are told that the martyrs in their triumph, all lucent, spoke their praise by the shore of a sea turned to glass. But the appearance, the face, the regard, the presence—what form the Holy One took, under what guise of splendor appeared—nothing is said. In other parts of Revelation, the Epiphany was a voice from throne or temple; in Exodus, an incandescent bush, a pillar of fire, a cloud.

Here they invoke the Holy One, in glory; and of that presence, not a word is said.

Yet they speak, *not* about, but *to* someone.

You alone are Holy.

I remember in another prison, we were allowed, in summer evenings, to sit on a small plot of grass in the jailyard. (Depending on the guards' moods, of course.) But in those hours of twilight, memories bring back to me the plaintive singing of a young prisoner and the welling of homesickness that stopped our voices and dried up our throats. That, and the beauty of a common weed, a dandelion in flower, a blade of grass weighed down by the peregrinations of an insect. The whole immense breadth of creation in small measure! Less is indeed more; we were undoing the American experience, which is systemically, by gigantism, appetite, feverish thrashing about (Polyphemus in a small garden), undoing creation.

Some sense of the holiness of all things came home to me in the moments I describe.

Are we not wise to treasure them? Realizing as well, and with considerable rue, that they come to us undeserved; but still, in a sense, deserved, when our lives bespeak reverence for living things?

I have ranged the earth and known many exacting and difficult moments, have seen every natural beauty, taken much to heart. But the holiness of things comes through to me, not in scenes of large compass where one is merely a kind of freeloader or tourist, but in the narrow breach; through a prison window, a knothole in a wooden cage, the sight of a barely surviving tree undergoing seasons of change; from another window the empty drama of clouds and sunny skies, everything reduced, seen through a burning glass.

One doesn't want to belabor a point harrowed back and forth by every psych who ever told fortunes by entrails, or put a nut pick to the divine mind.

Holiness? Another name for God.

Another name for us? Like lighting a torch from the sun: "Be you perfect as God is perfect."

Choose to be chosen.

A new command I give you: love one another as I have loved you.

Heaven and earth are filled with your glory.

Sometimes one thinks: what an easy, attractive offer, that we line up our lives with the divine—many cards aligned with the king of hearts.

Those are the elusive moments: the mere thought of holiness, the image of Jesus thrown on the cave wall by the flowery hands of children.

Children! The journey stops at a cave door, abruptly.

There, the fire casts no rune. Even the shadowy mime dissolves.

Here in this spacey ship of fools I feel about as holy as a stinking mop rag. Life has all the splendiferous aura of an open privy.

[99]

Holy, Holy? Bend your ear to the chorus, a scratchy record in a groove; the minds of prisoners shuffle about, wall to wall on run-down heels. . . .

My case, my lawyer, this dude, that freak. S.O.B. judge. The fuzz said to me. Lewisburg. Got to beat this rap. Bum rap. You know it. Gotta smoke to spare? Mother fuckin' guard. Like I say, if I can beat this one. . . .

This is the universal language of the submerged, the sign language of the dead. It is, of course, closely aped, even though sanitized, cleverized, relevantized by practically all who, never having been in the slammer, think of themselves habitually as good citizens, masters of reality, good Bible Christians, good lawyers, judges, professors, clerics. Those cunning weavers and dyers of the web in which, to be sure, dumb flies are entangled and perish.

But that is a diversion. Why pursue the single dark thread of the web, to learn from whose guts it is concocted—is this an attack on the language of decent men and women? (Only insofar as their language is an attack on the holiness of God.) Which, of course, brings us to the question of the language of worship. It is a common understanding that praise of the holiness of God is spoken largely to our credit, bounces great waves of merit off us like hailstones off a bronze hero in the park. One truth however is largely ignored; that witnesses of the holiness of God don't normally get statues raised in public places.

Allow me to say, I have no confidence in the supposition that the Holy ones by the sea of glass were merely articulating the common understanding of Church or State

with regard to the great You
who among believers is commonly regarded

as a He
out there somewhere (out of sight, out of mind)
is here somewhere
(head trip, heart trip, space trip)
or more commonly—
an inert It (just next door to the Id),
an empty bronze, self-cast, self-modeled, self-fired
horse, mount, a magnificent leap of Ego; and presto!
    heaved to its pedestal.
the self in question being our own, not God's.
In sum I suggest (my present circumstance, which is jail
is my biology, which is my destiny)
that most of the time the cry of Holy, Holy, Holy
is by no means
a flame struck from those holy spirits.
It is rather a sickly
quasi-military
spasmodic autistic
salute
                to ourselves, our web; our tortured insects even
(who secrete a kind of ambrosia for the gods),
                the hanged dried out carcasses, proof
that the rebellion is indeed quelled,
the powers dominant
the principalities (as heretofore)
strictly in command.

If You alone are holy
what are we to make of ourselves?
Alas, the biblical word is in accord
with the facts of life—
a moonlight gentle as outpoured milk, a libation

on a rifled tomb.
Not much.
Except the spilt milk gathers itself
in the moon's silver pitcher
held by no human hand
to the lips of the resurrected; they
climb from their tombs hand over hand,
thirsty with long dusty bone scattering sleep.

All the Nations Will Come and Worship Before You

And they say scripture is not political! It is in fact political, as it is the nature of God to be political (hence the three persons in conjunction of life, creation, vision) as we are in fact political (born of the human line; our first political act, getting born; our second, our first milky meal; very nearly our third, giving birth, in the multiple sense required, to an idea, a poem, a child).

In any case, scripture deals with unlikelihoods. And of all unlikely events, the present one ought to be celebrated: the submission of the nations. So unlikely that time could well tick its way into eternity without its occurring.

Meantime, the substitute occurrences, which is to say, the nations that never come "to worship before him," are continually, supposedly, by prior arrangement and public fanfare, coming to worship before him. They come in procession, toward the Churches, i.e., the national Churches. They come as "Christian" nations; the concordats signed, the mutual duties and rights and interests secured. Only the most jaundiced and ungenerous minds, the most atheistically tinged and inhumanly stingy spirits could fail to sense the great benefit accruing, in all directions, from such ar-

rangements. As though a pope were scattering gold coins—stamped on one side with the image of Christ, on the other, the image of Caesar—from his balcony. He is like the sun, the sun of justice, his bounty falls indiscriminate and majestic, on all comers. Are there murmurers in the crowd, defectors, complainers, even a sour-faced atheist, a communist in a fool's red cap? No matter, he may also catch a coin, the sun's arm is long as day, generous as noon . . . though he spit on the coin like a mean fox and bite it like a parrot, it will bring luck to his children—or a great loaf of bread.

The key of the Kingdom of heaven is not a long shaft, ending in a cunning metal jigsaw cutout, *chi* and *rho*; no, it ends in a coin simple and round and two-faced: Caesar and Christ. Infinitely precious because of the second, whose business is eternity; infinitely (one must not hesitate at the adverb) useful in the necessary buying and selling, opening and shutting, persuading and disclaiming, forgiving and retaining, protecting and repelling, delating and denying, bribing (even) and silencing, which are the proper business of a Church installed (by Christ himself it is said) in this world.

Before the humans came the apes, according to a celebrated theory.

An application of which to the present subject might read: before the human (fully human) formal and final act envisioned in our prayer—the worship of God by the nations of the earth—before this, came a whole sauntering chattering procession, vaguely aping what was to come.

What was to come was simply an act of God. "For the healing of the nations." The prayer is not a prayer within history, no matter how often it is said, repeated, memorized by heart, chanted in whatever tongues, by whatever races. All this, with respect to the prayer of the blessed in eternity, is a prehuman act. For the fully human

act, we must await an act of God. Welcome to the gate of ivory, otherwise called "the shore of the sea of glass."

Meantime, say I, let the nations go about their proper business, which is predictable and lethal as, say, the birth of the next nuclear warhead. The business is death. In our lifetime, to the infinite satisfaction of the nations, business is good.

One way of putting the present Christian difficulty: we are trying to say, let the nation go about its proper business. But don't try to induct us into it. Now this implies two cheerful conclusions, here freely offered to fellow (sister) Christians, a red apple in a hollow time.

1) Suppose that large (or even small) numbers of Christians began to feel a pricking in their thumbs at the unwarranted intrusion of the nation's snout (it has a nose for death) into their Bible ("Thou shalt not kill"). Why then the national nose, which grows like Pinocchio's in sniffing out others' affairs, might pull back.

2) And in such an effort, Christians might well recover their eyesight, and the light to read by. The first removing an inhibition (the State exegete reading the text for us, bending it to imperial use) and the second removing a prohibition of the Spirit: our true light and advocate, who seems to absent himself from our scene, as long as present arrangements prevail.

Because Your Righteous Deeds are Seen by All!

——When will such a thing come to pass, that your deeds are seen by all?

——You will never see it come to pass.

——Then how am I to know it will occur at all?

——You take someone's word for it.

——You realize what you're asking. I'm sitting on ice here in ol' Virginny where the cotton and the corn and 'taters grow. I'm here because at least one or two of God's righteous deeds were seen by a few of us. Now you come by, like the pill pusher here with his pieman's tray, and you hand out your narcotic: upper or downer or both.

——It's not a pill, it's a prophecy. There's a difference, you'll recall.

——I hadn't finished. Maybe you have in mind a day when jailer and jailed change places? I'll be outside jangling keys and slamming doors and generally harassing my harasser? It doesn't sound very inviting to me.

——No, that wasn't the idea, or even near to it. What I had in mind was a day when inside and outside would melt away like wax candles or be whisked away like the flimsiest veil. Each in the other. Each pregnant with the other, pressing upon the other, not I to become you or you me; but each to remain pressingly, ripely, terminally, the other.

——You mean I'm to respect the powers that turn locks on me here, want to turn me into a demented animal?

——I don't want to make a prisoner's lot any more bitter than it has to be. But look: no one's claiming the guard-prisoner ratio of insight is anything like fifty-fifty. Even if it were true, that kind of numbers game stinks of war, not salvation. The ratio may well be ninety-eight to two in your favor. Still, I submit that's just as irrelevant to the point that scripture is making, as though your jailer were named Peter of the Keys and you, Judas of the Purse.

——Now that's an intriguing idea. Maybe those are our real names.

——Real, surreal. The point of scripture is intact. Namely, the day any humans get to see an act of God, is a day known to God. It is not a day of goodwill industries, or of American know-how or of Harvard genius, or of the raining down of Nobel prizes. It is not even a day of heroism or a day of martyrdom. Nor a day tolled by Swedish design or imagined by Latin seers. Nor the day of the iguana, nor the day of the Rockefellers. Need I say not the day of awards for fervent civic virtue; not even the day of atonement? Pile the achievement high as the heavens, sink the pilings deep, deep. Let the Te Deums ring out the latest sordid military murders. I'll go further. Let the martyrs cry out from their cells under the altar of sacrifice. He'll do no more even for those beloved ones, than cast them a gnawed bone. "Patience, be patient!" The word cast in the teeth of every folly and achievement and structure and triumph and definitive solution and war on cancer and misspent or well spent bullet is the same word. Not yet. Not by a long shot.

——At least you can ask him something on my behalf. Ask him when I get out of here.

——I did. He said to tell you, not yet.